A COLORING BOOK FOR THE LA

COLOR-X

RAMP SURFACE SKATELITE

FOREWARD

"DO IT, AND DO IT EXCEPTIONALLY."

WELCOME TO THE OFFICIAL SKATELITE COLORING BOOK, A FUN AND UNIQUE PRODUCT THAT ENCOURAGES CREATIVITY AND TELLS OUR STORY.

RICHLITE WAS CREATED IN 1943, MARKING THE BEGINNING OF A LEGACY STEEPED IN CRAFTSMANSHIP, RESILIENCE AND INNOVATION. SINCE SKATELITE'S ENTRY INTO ACTION SPORTS IN 1995, WE'VE BECOME A SYMBOL OF PASSION AND PROGRESS; A PROMISE TO ATHLETES WORLDWIDE THAT THE METICULOUSLY CRAFTED MATERIAL THEY ARE PERFORMING ON WILL STAND THE TEST OF TIME. IT'S A TESTAMENT TO A TRADITION WE'VE BUILT OVER DECADES WHERE QUALITY IS VALUED ABOVE ALL; WHERE THE ART OF PERFECTION, THE FIRE OF CREATION AND THE THRILL OF UNMATCHED QUALITY CONVERGE.

WITH THAT TRADITION IN MIND, WE'VE TEAMED UP WITH OUR FRIENDS AT COLOR-X TO CRAFT THIS EPIC BOOK OF FUN ACTIVITIES, BRAND TRIVIA AND THE MOST LEGENDARY MOMENTS THAT HAVE TAKEN PLACE ON OUR PRODUCTS.

SO GET YOUR BOARDS AND COLORED PENCILS READY. IT'S GONNA BE A WILD, (AND SMOOTH) RIDE THANKS TO THE WORLD'S MOST DURABLE AND TRUSTED SURFACES... SKATELITE!

HERE'S TO PUSHING FORWARD,

WORD VERT

```
Y I K D C O M M U N I T Y S F N Y V V Y
F P A P E R K I S H Z O S C P L C W O X
S E R E C Y C L E D F Y K R K F I E W D
T U S T W E Y M O J G S A A D S H T Y U
W E S G F J G C S A X T T F O C F V Z R
F B A T H H B P I U T Y E T D C W Q M A
X U B F A R M D Q Y G R L S U E O L C B
S R S G O I X X Y C Z E I M P R E Z A L
W D K U K C N E G U V S T A S T Q O R E
P E R F O R M A N C E I E N U I M I D S
F L T W F R G B B B Q L G S R F N L B M
N D W C X F A C U L E I N H F I N U O O
Z W J W F Q M M P N E E H I A E A S A O
G X G J L T U F P M X N Z P C D Z F R T
J R S T O N Z H B R G T V H E O W S D H
```

SKATELITE
PAPER
SMOOTH
RECYCLED
FSCCERTIFIED

DURABLE
PERFORMANCE
SURFACE
CARDBOARD
CRAFTSMANSHIP

COMMUNITY
SUSTAINABLE
BMX
RESILIENT
RAMP

SKATELITE SNOW WALLRIDE

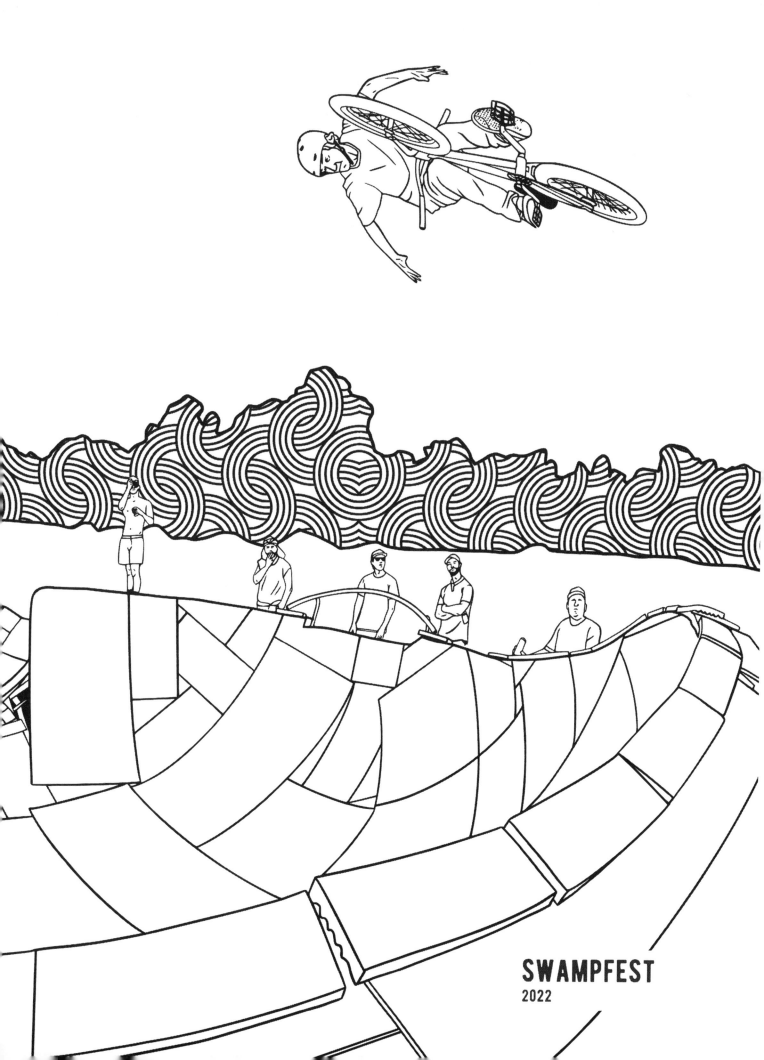

SEEING THINGS

FIND THE DIFFERENCES IN THE SKATERS. THEN LIST THEM BELOW.

1 _____
2 _____
3 _____
4 _____

CROSSWORD

ACROSS

2. Skatelite is made from recycled_____ .
3. Danny Way jumped the Great_____ of China on Skatelite in 2005.
4. Skatelite is the leading choice to_____ your ramp from Mother Nature's elements.
6. We are based in_____ , Washington in the same building where it all started.
7. Skatelite is a_____ owned and operated company since 1995.
8. Skatelite is_____ proof of up to 350 degrees.

DOWN

1. 12 year old Gui Khury is the first person to land a 1080 on_____ ramp on Skatelite.
3. Skatelite is 100%_____ proof so no need to worry about rain.
5. Our parent company_____ , was founded in 1943.
8. Tony_____ landed the first 900 on Skatelite at the 1999 X-Games.

UNSCRAMBLE
MAKE SENSE OF THESE WORDS, DUDE

PARM _____

ESTAK _____

ECSUAFR _____

RADEBLU _____

DERSH _____

EVITRN _____

TESIEKLAT _____

RAPPE _____

RABDOCRAD _____

YECLECRD _____

LIRACAD _____

NAMPREROCEF _____

STEVE CABALLERO
@STEVECABALLERO

ANSWER KEY

SEEING THINGS
FIND THE DIFFERENCES IN THE SKATERS. THEN LIST THEM BELOW.

1. Top of the hat is black
2. Eyebrows are tilted down
3. Top axle screw is clear
4. Shoe logo is a circle

WORD VERT

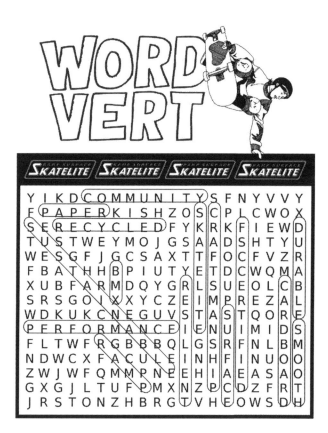

UNSCRAMBLE
MAKE SENSE OF THESE WORDS, DUDE

PARM	Ramp
ESTAK	Skate
ECSUAFR	Surface
RADEBLU	Durable
DERSH	Shred
EVITRN	Invert
TESIEKLAT	Skatelite
RAPPE	Paper
RABDOCRAD	Cardboard
YECLECRD	Recycled
LIRACAD	Radical
NAMPREROCEF	Performance

CROSSWORD

Across:
2. PAPER
3. WALL
4. PROTECT
6. TACOMA
7. FAMILY
8. HEAT

Down:
1. VERT
3. WATER
5. RICH / SKATELITE
8. HAWK

ANSWER KEY

CONTRIBUTORS

ATHLETES
STEVE CABALLERO
CHRISTIAN HOSOI
LIZZIE ARMANTO
GAVIN LILLER
CHRIS HIETT
COCO ZURITA
BRYCE WETTSTEIN
ELLIOT SLOAN
MIKE CRUM
NATE WESSEL
DARREN NAVARRETTE
MIKE FRAZIER
MAT HOFFMAN
REGGIE KELLY
ZION CLARK

SKATELITE TEAM
MELISSA HUSTON
CHAD FOREMAN
WILL OWENS
KEVIN MARQUEZ
DAXTER LUSSIER

ILLUSTRATORS
MATT CANTRELL
ERIC ECKERT

PHOTOGRAPHERS
WILL OWENS
CHAD FOREMAN

COLOR-X TEAM
GANTRY HILL
GARRETT HILL

PRODUCERS
SKATELITE
MELISSA HUSTON
COLOR-X BOOKS

DESIGNERS
ANDREW BRASWELL
GANTRY HILL

SKATELITE IS A REGISTERED TRADEMARK OF RICHLITE, 2023. COLOR-X IS A REGISTERED TRADEMARK OF COLOR-X BOOKS, 2023.
SOME PATTERNS WERE DESIGNED WITH ASSETS FROM FREEPIK.COM.